The Good Idea

by Katherine Scraper
illustrated by Anthony Lewis

"I have a broom," said Pam.

"I have trash bags," said Dad.
"We can help clean the park."

3

"Look! Ron is at the park," said Pam. "I see him at the fountain. Can Ron help us?"

"We can go and see,"
said Dad.

Pam said, "Are you here to help clean the park, Ron?"

Ron had a sad face.

"I can not help," said Ron. "I have no broom. I have no net. See the trash? I can not get it."

"I have an idea," said Pam.

"Dad, can Ron use the net?"

"Yes," Dad said. "That is a good idea!"

"You can dip it in, Ron," said Pam. "Can you get the trash?"

"I can! I can!" said Ron.

Dot said, "You had a
good idea, Pam."

"There is no trash now," said Pam.

"I have a good idea. I have juice for you. I have fruit bars for you," said Dad.

"The papers go in the trash," said Ron.

"The cans go in here!" said Pam.

"It is fun to clean the park," said Ron and Pam.

"Yes, it is," said Dad.